USING MATHS VOCABULARY

Dictionary

for 5–7 year olds

Heinemann
Halley Court, Jordan Hill, Oxford, OX2 8EJ
a division of Reed Educational and Professional Publishing Ltd
www.heinemann.co.uk

Heinemann is a registered trademark of
Reed Educational and Professional Publishing Ltd

First published 2001

ISBN 0435 186728

06 05 04 03 02 01
10 9 8 7 6 5 4 3 2 1

Designed by Jonathan Williams
Illustrated by Simone Abel, Oxford Illustrators and Jonathan Williams

Printed and bound by Edelvives, Zaragoza

USING MATHS VOCABULARY

Dictionary

for 5–7 year olds

David Kirkby

a b c d e f g h i j k l m n o p q r s t u v w x y z

add, addition See also: operation

You **add** things when you find the **total** of two or more numbers.

+ This is an **addition** or **plus** sign.

3 + 4 = 7

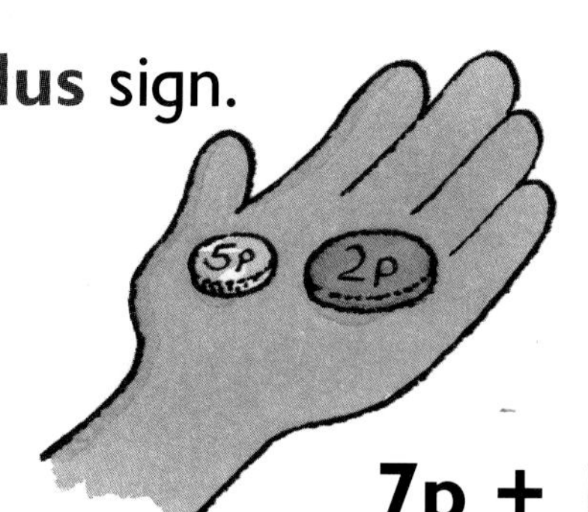

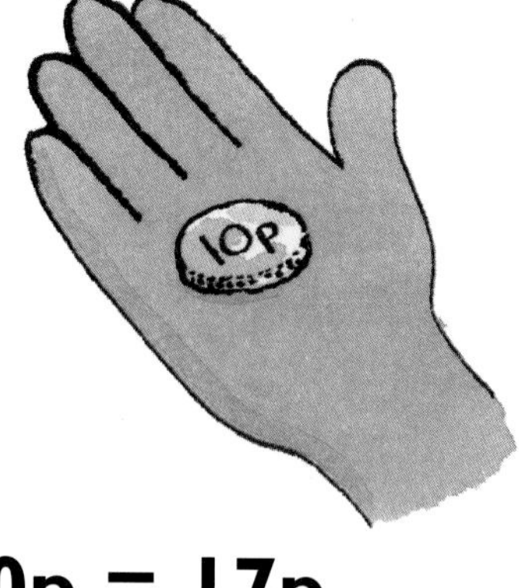

7p + 10p = 17p

These are additions.
Addition is the opposite of **subtraction**.

analogue clock

An **analogue clock** has two hands to show the time.
It has a **minute** hand and an **hour** hand.
The minute hand is **longer** than the hour hand.

The time is seven o'clock.

anti-clockwise See also: clockwise

Anti-clockwise is the opposite direction to the way the hands of a clock move.

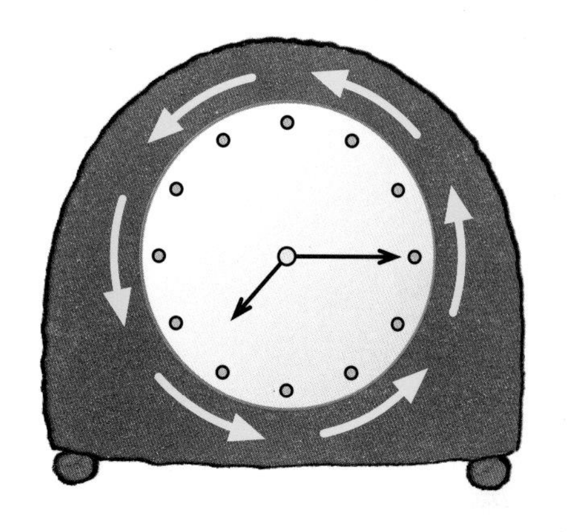

anti-clockwise

array

Arrays are made from **rows** and **columns.**

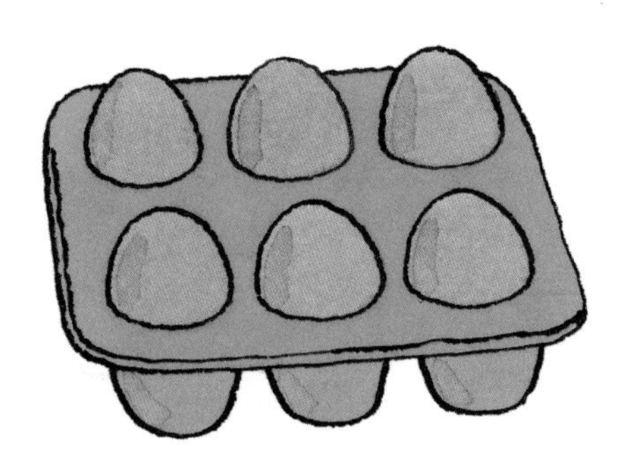

2 rows and 3 columns.

3 rows and 5 columns.

balance

When two things **weigh** the same amount they **balance.**

block graph

See also: graph

A **block graph** shows information about amounts of things using blocks.

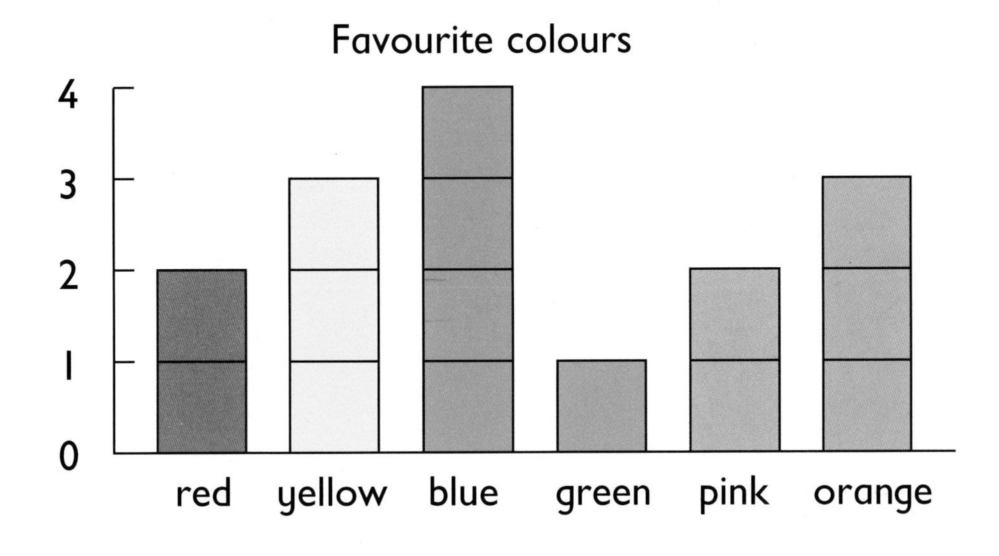

a
b
c
d
e
f
g
h
i
j
k
l
m
n
o
p
q
r
s
t
u
v
w
x
y
z

calculate, calculation

See also: operation, mental

You **calculate** when you work out something.

These are **calculations**.

capacity

Capacity is the amount a container will hold. You **measure** capacity in **litres** and **millilitres**.

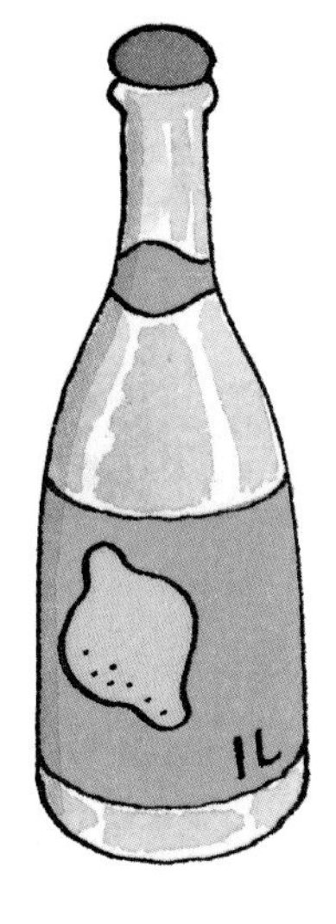

The capacity of this bottle is 1 litre (1 l).

centimetre

A **centimetre** is a **measure** of **length**.

The marks on this ruler are
one centimetre apart.
The finger is 5 centimetres **long**.

cm is short for centimetre.
100 centimetres is a **metre**.

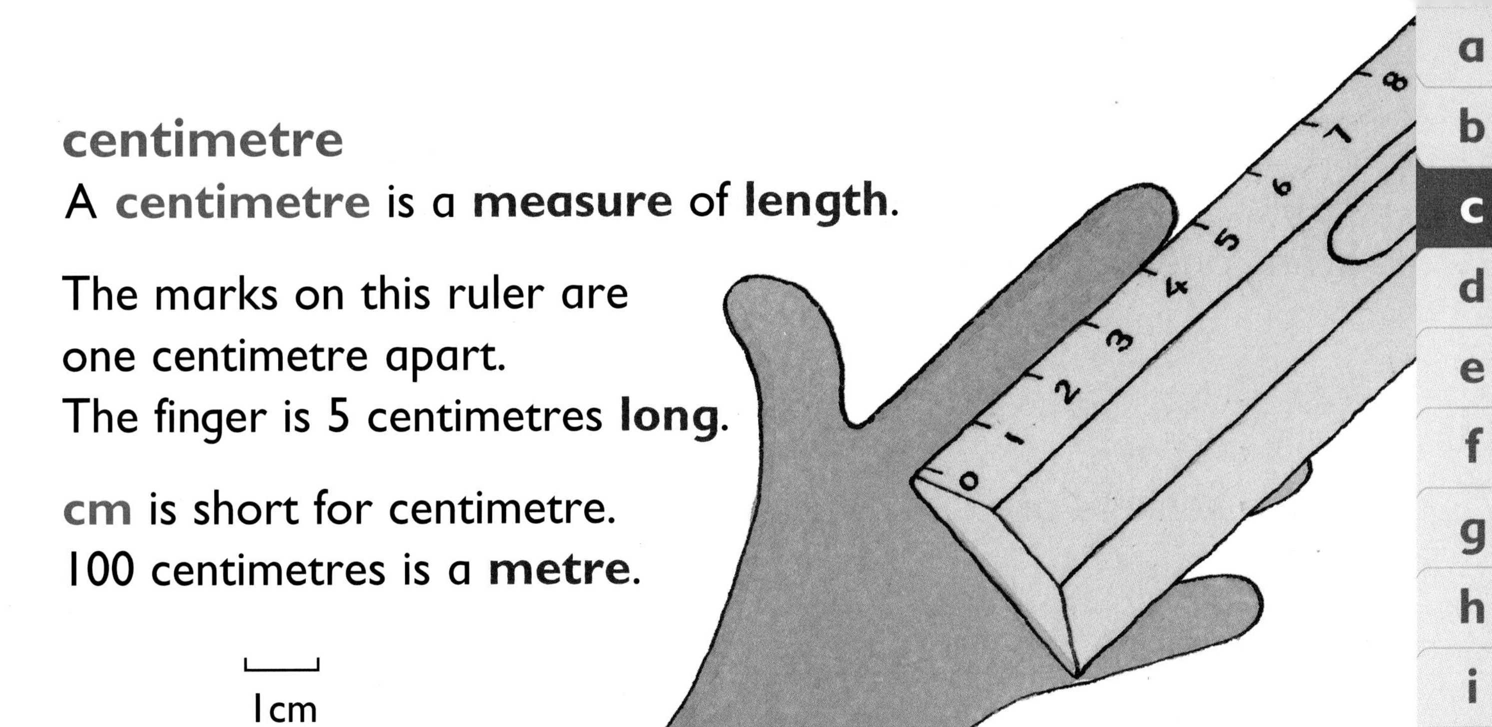

centre

The **centre** is the middle
point of a shape or object.

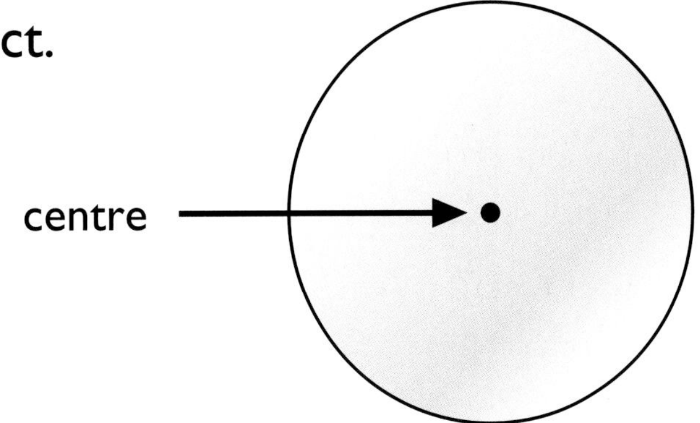

change

You get **change** when you pay
for an object with a **coin** of a higher value.

a b c d e f g h i j k l m n o p q r s t u v w x y z

circle, circular

A **circle** is a perfectly round shape.
It has one **curved side**.

These stickers are **circular**. They are circle shaped.

clockwise **See also: anti-clockwise**

The hands of a clock move in a **clockwise** direction.

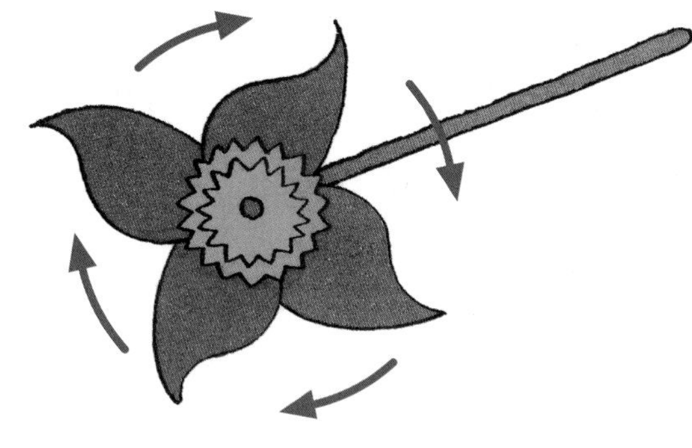

coin

Coins are money.
Coins are worth 1p, 2p, 5p, 10p, 20p, 50p, £1 or £2.

column **See also: array**

A **column** is a line of objects or **numbers**, one above the other.

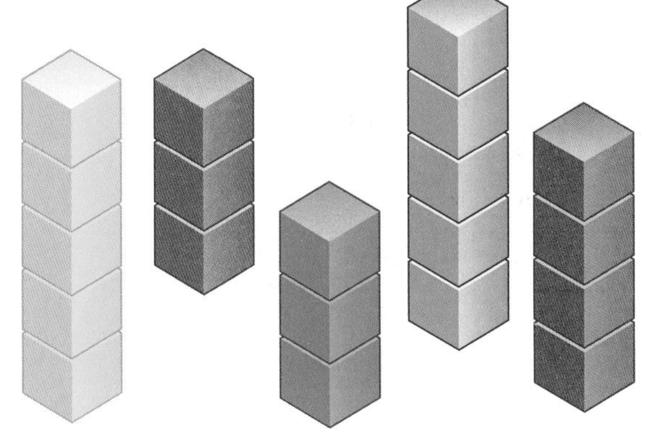

Five columns of bricks.

Zac	Sal	Jan	Amy
4	3	2	1
1	4	0	3
2	1	3	4
3	2	0	1
5	0	4	2

A chart with four columns.

cone

A **cone** is a solid shape with one pointed end and one **circular** end.

corner

A **corner** is where the **sides** or **edges** of a shape meet.

corners

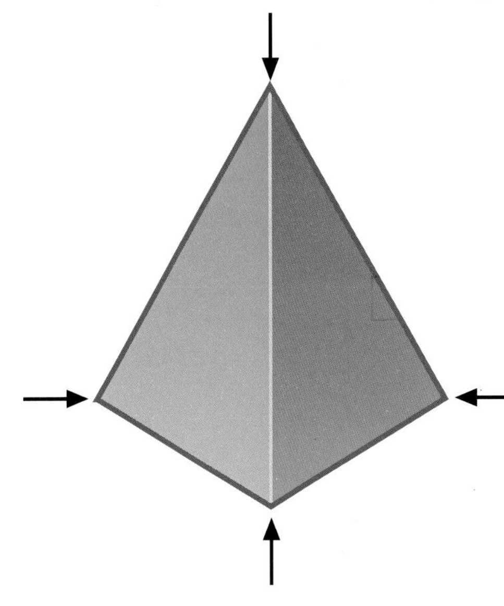

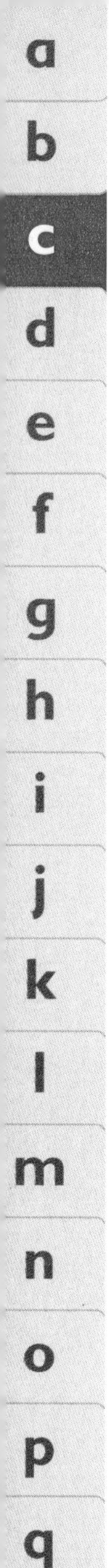

cube

A **cube** is a **solid** shape.
Cubes have 6 **square faces**.
All the faces are the same size.

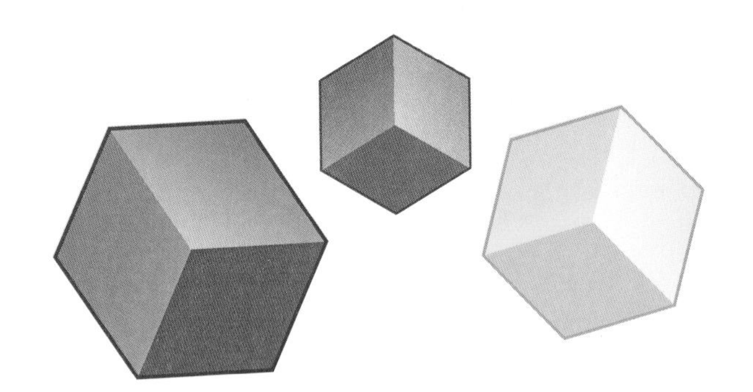

cuboid

A **cuboid** is a solid shape with 6 **rectangular faces**.
Most boxes are cuboids.

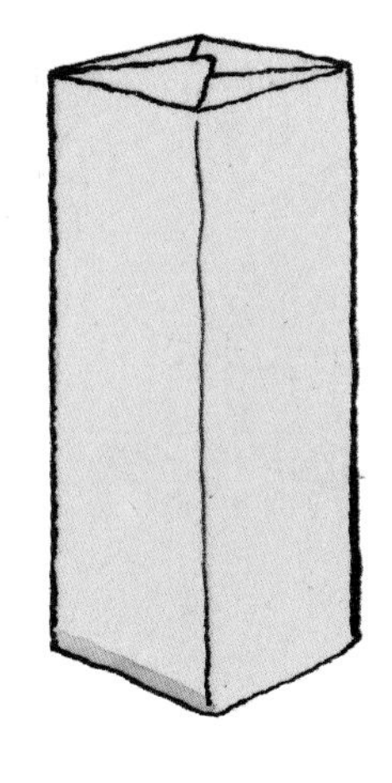

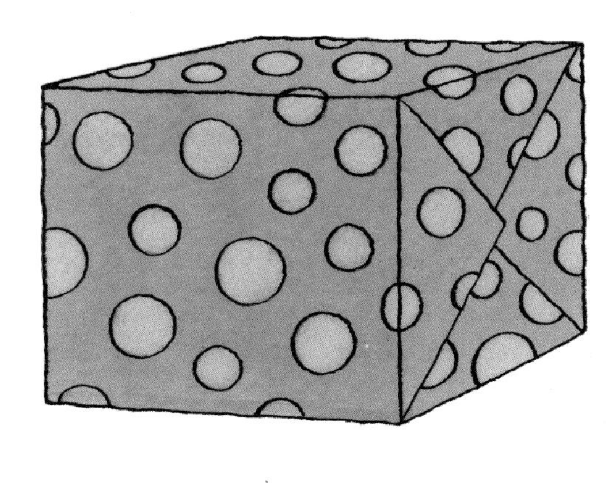

curved

A **curved line** is not **straight**.
These lines are curved.

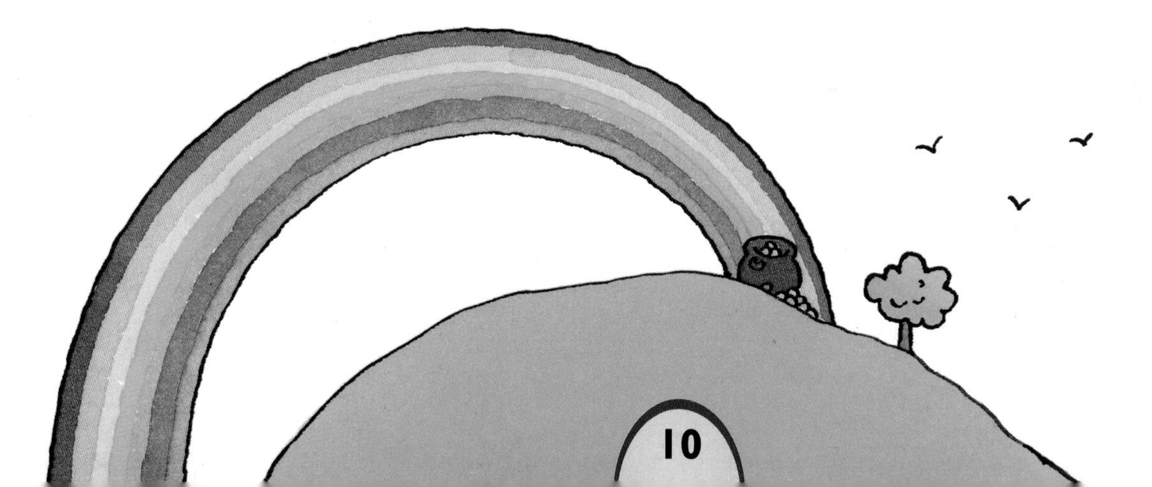

cylinder

A **cylinder** is a **solid** shape with a **circular face** at each end and a **curved** face between.

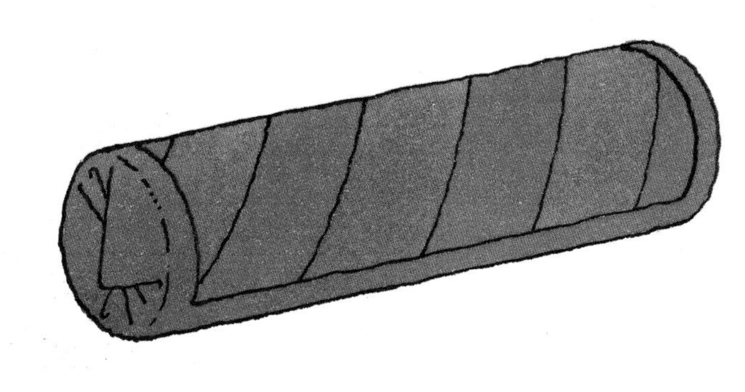

day

See also: month, tomorrow, yesterday

A **day** is 24 **hours** long.
There are seven days in a **week**.

difference

The **difference** between two **numbers** is how much **more** or **less** one is than the other.

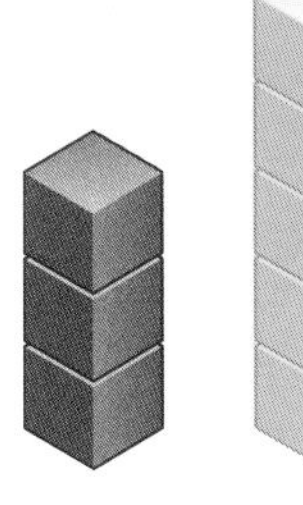
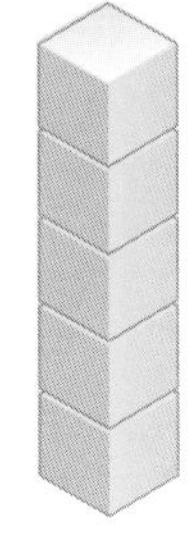

The difference between 3 and 5 is 2.

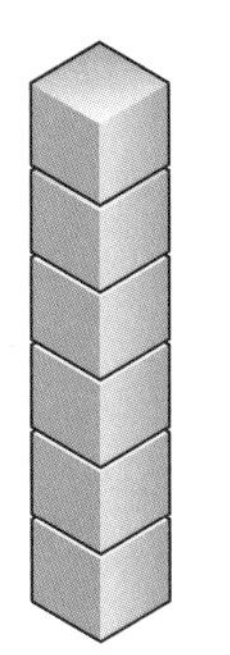
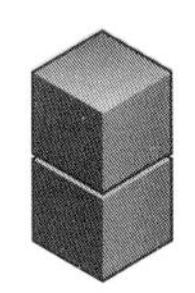

The difference between 6 and 2 is 4.

digit

See also: digital clock, place value, three-digit number, two-digit number

A **digit** is one of the counting **numbers:**
0, 1, 2, 3, 4, 5, 6, 7, 8, 9.

These are digit cards.

digital clock

A **digital clock** uses **digits** to show the time.

divide, divided by, division

See also: operation

You **divide** when you share or group things into equal **sets**.

÷ This sign means **'divided by'**.

The 8 biscuits have been divided by 2.
They are shared into 2 groups
with 4 biscuits in each.

8 ÷ 2 = 4

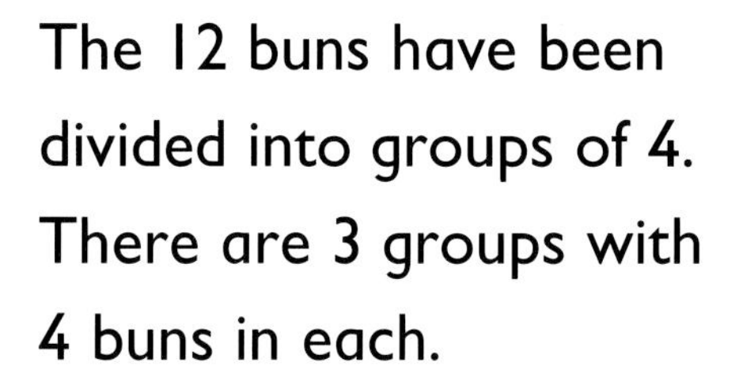

The 12 buns have been
divided into groups of 4.
There are 3 groups with
4 buns in each.

12 ÷ 4 = 3

Division is the opposite
of **multiplication**.

double

Double a **number** is two times the number,
or **twice** the number.

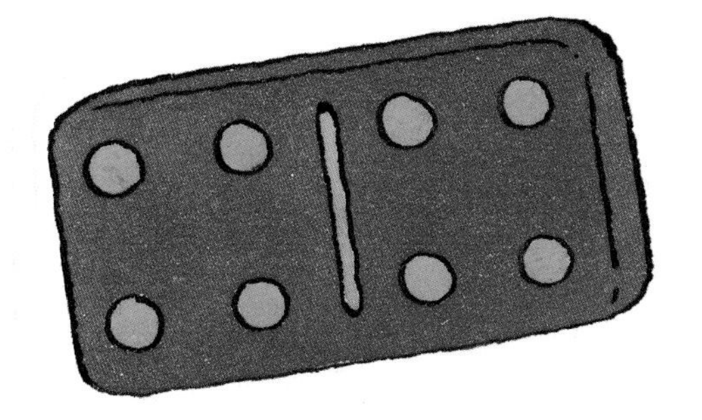

Double 4 is 8.

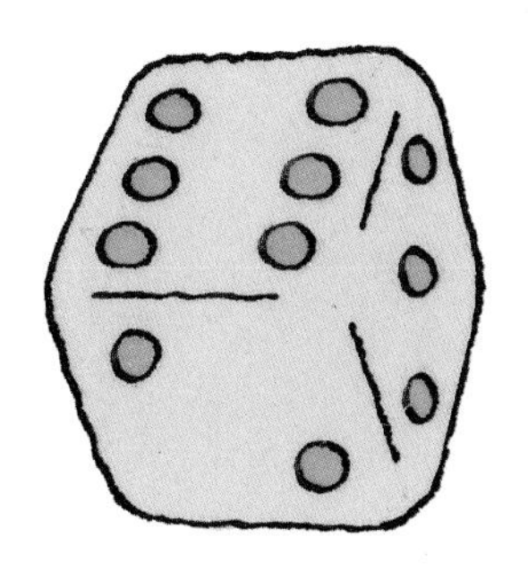

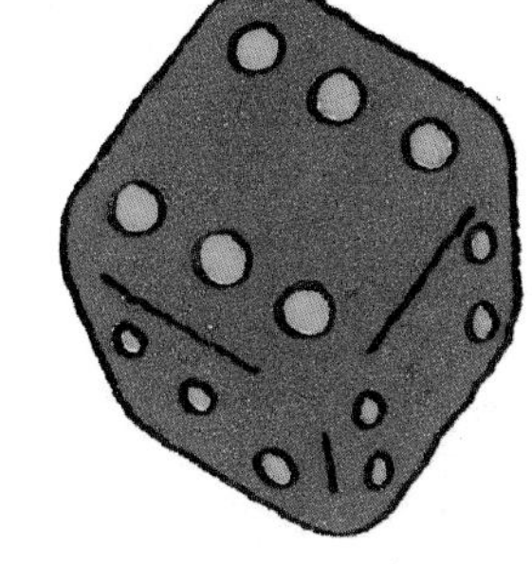

Double 6 is 12.

edge

Solid shapes have **edges** where two **faces** meet.

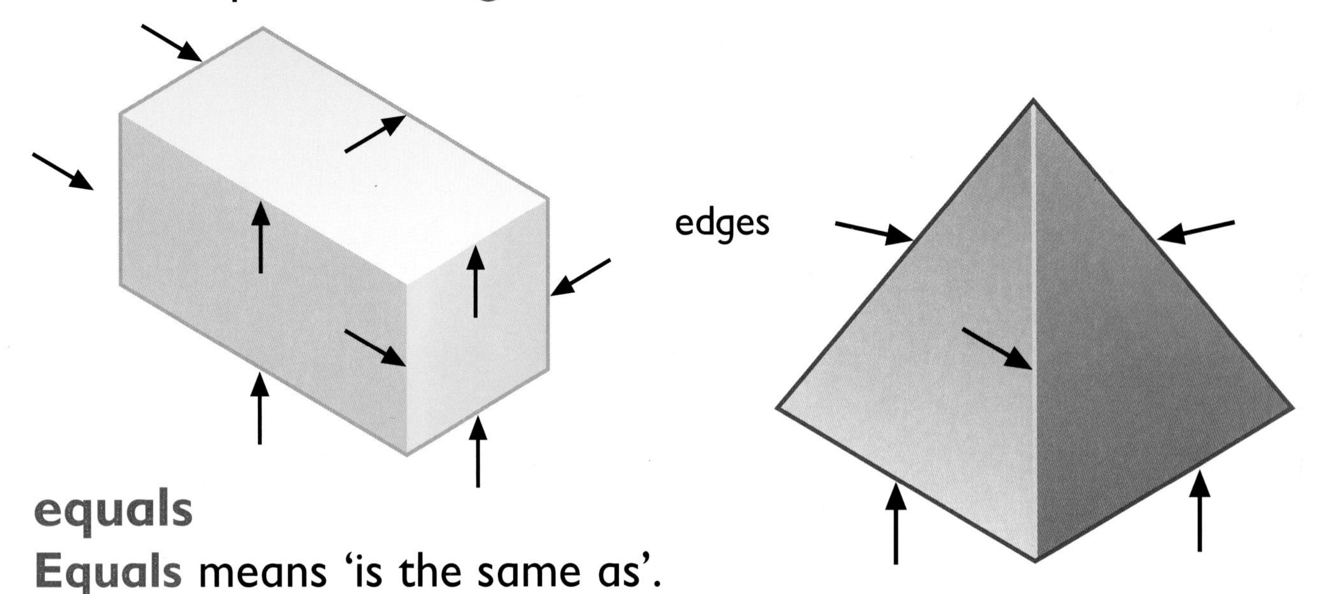

equals

Equals means 'is the same as'.

= This is an equals sign.

estimate

An **estimate** is a good guess to decide how much.

How **long**? About 5 **centimetres**.

How much? About £1.

How many? About 70.

even number

An **even number** can be **divided** exactly by two.

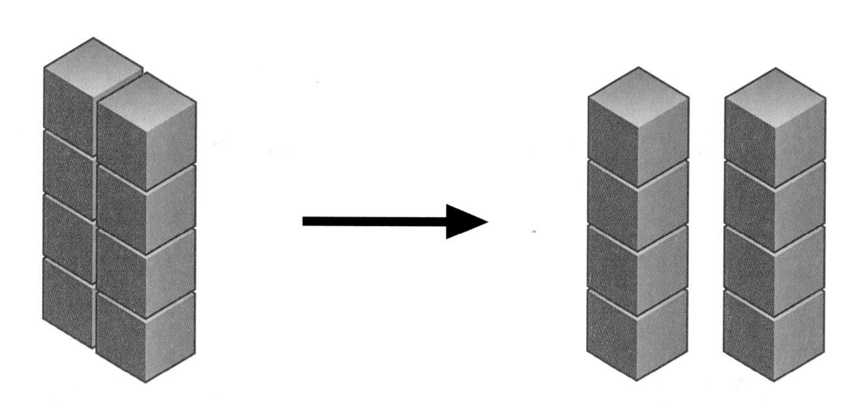

These are even numbers.
The missing numbers are **odd numbers**.

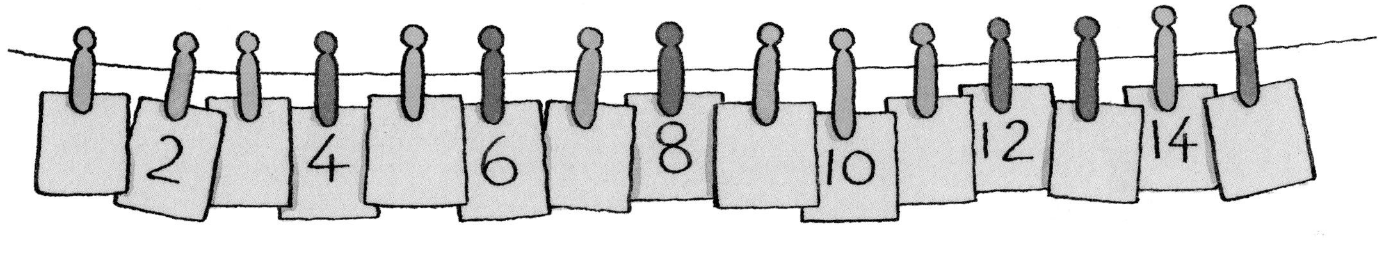

face

Solid shapes have **faces**.
They can be **flat** or **curved**.

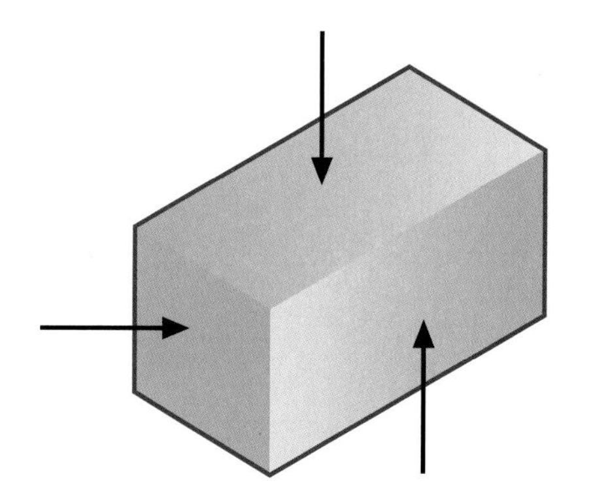

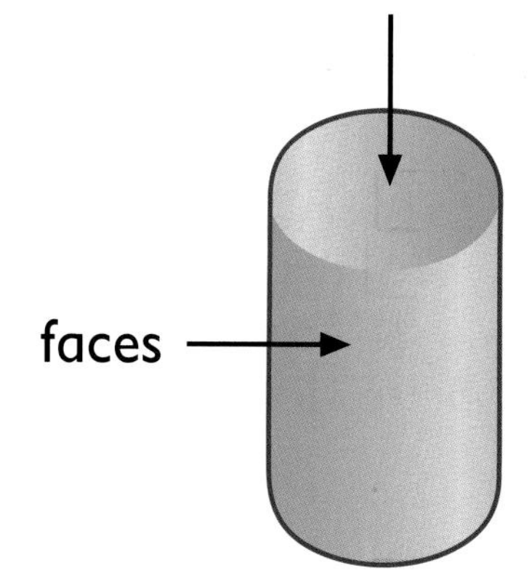

few, fewer, fewest

Few means small in **number**, not many.

Pip has **fewer** spots than Ross.
Ross has fewer spots than Sam.
Pip has **fewest** spots.

a b c d e f g h i j k l m n o p q r s t u v w x y z

flat **See also: corner, side**

These are **flat** shapes. They have **length** and width but no thickness.

fortnight

A **fortnight** is 2 **weeks** or 14 **days**.

A fortnight to go!

fraction

A **fraction** is part of a whole one.

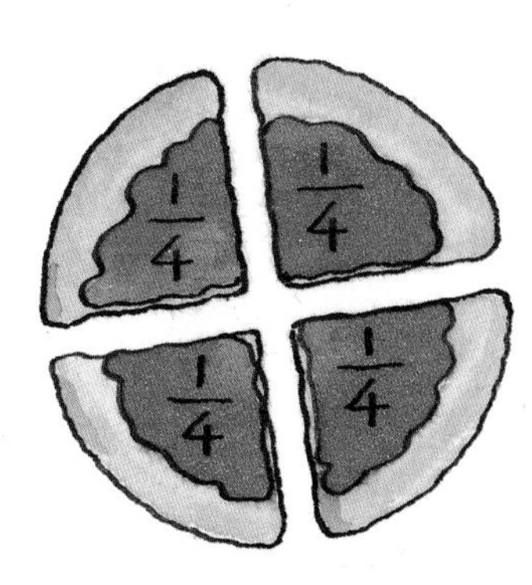

Each piece is a fraction of the whole one.

gram

A **gram** is a **measure** of **weight**.

g is short for gram.
1000 grams is a **kilogram**.

graph **See also: pictogram, block graph**

A **graph** is a chart that shows information about amounts of things.

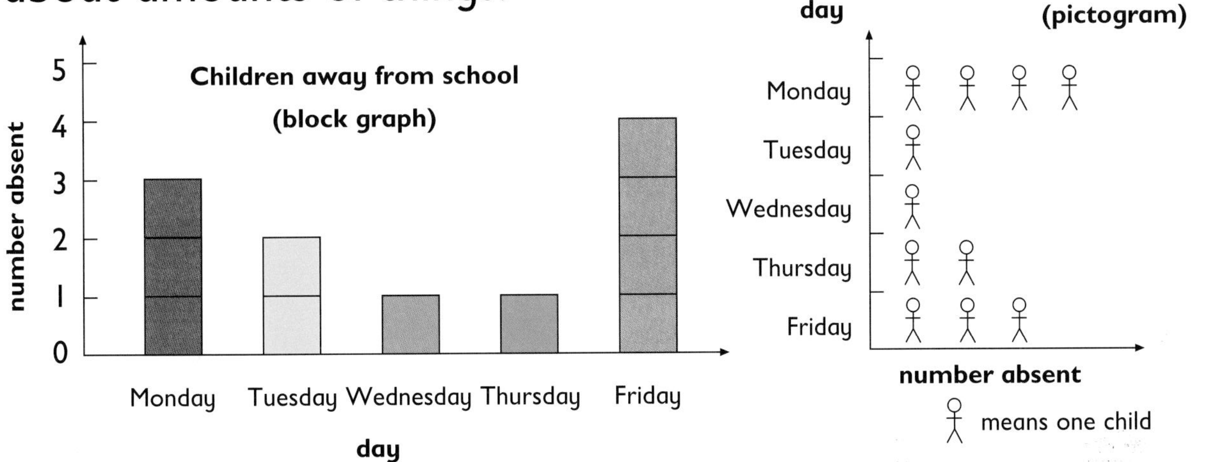

half, halve **See also: half past, half turn**

Each of these is a **half**.
A half is a **fraction**.
There are two halves in a whole.

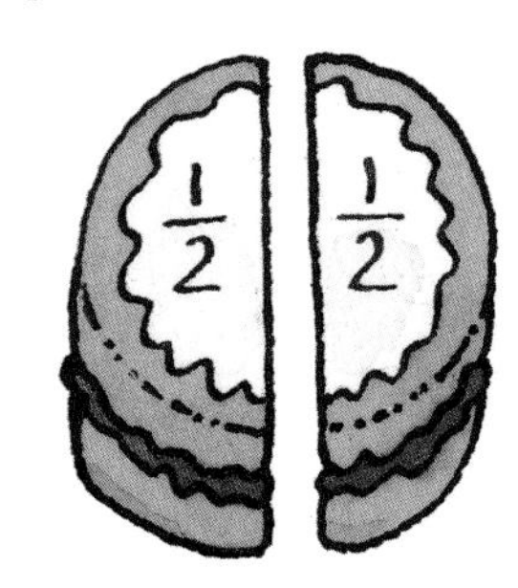

When you **halve** something, you **divide** it into two equal parts.

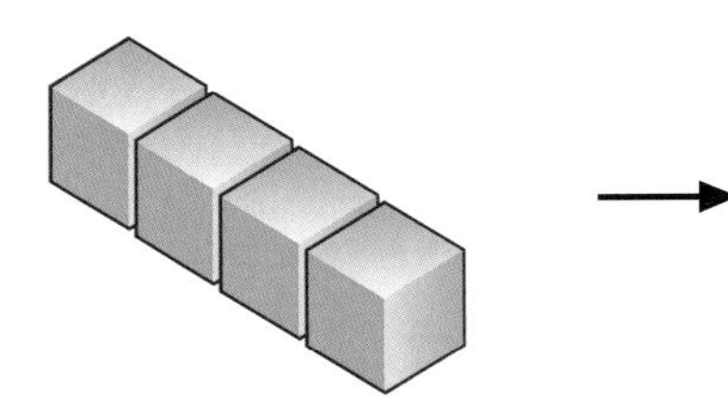

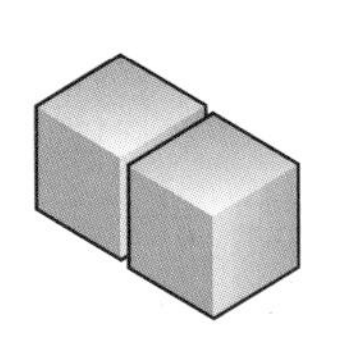

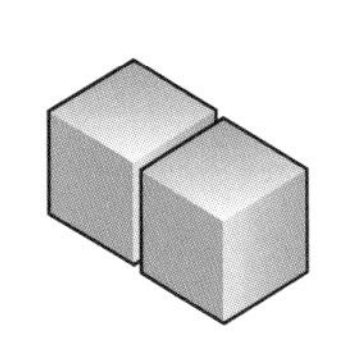

a b c d e f g h i j k l m n o p q r s t u v w x y z

a b c d e f g h i j k l m n o p q r s t u v w x y z

half past

Half past means half way between two 'o'clock' times.
It is 30 minutes past the hour.

half past two

half turn

A **half turn** is a half
of a **whole turn.**
Two half turns make
one whole turn.

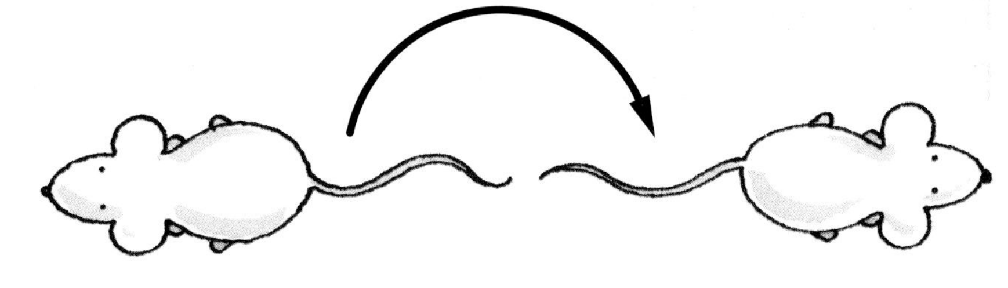

heavy, heavier, heaviest

Heavy means having a lot of **weight**.

The bear is **heavier** than the adult.
The adult is heavier than the child.
The bear is the **heaviest**.

hexagon

A **hexagon** has 6 **straight sides** and 6 **corners**.

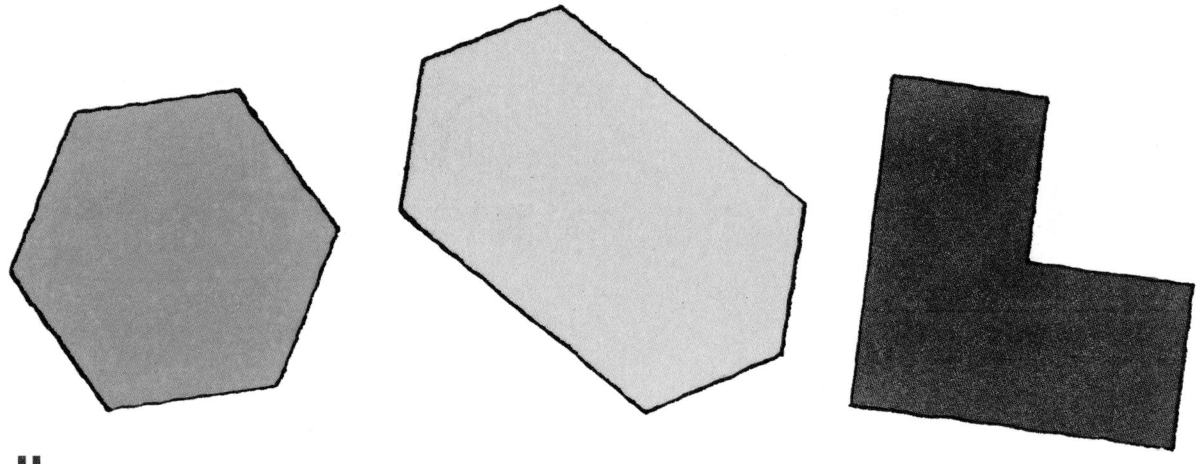

hollow

These shapes are **hollow**.
They have space inside. They are not **solid**.

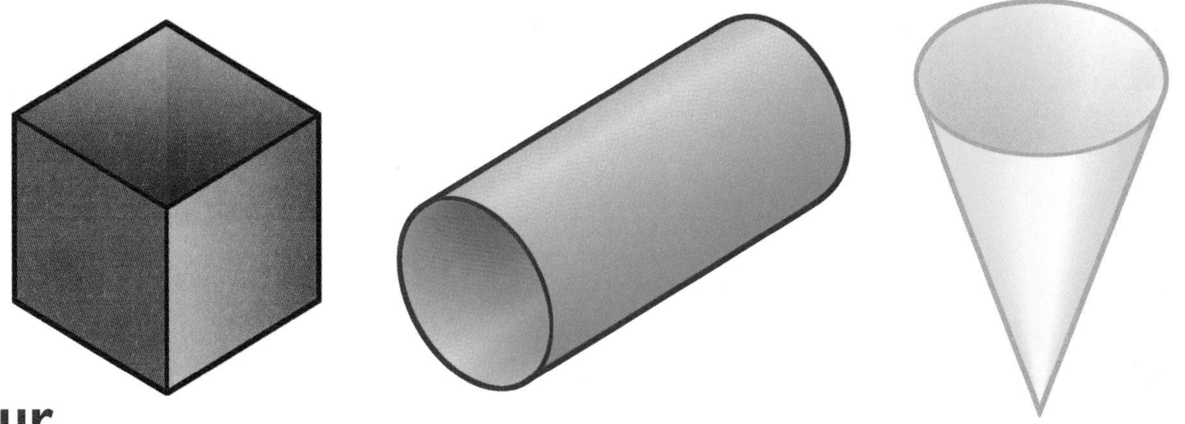

hour

An **hour** is a **measure** of time. An hour is 60 **minutes** long.
There are 24 hours in a **day**.

hundred, hundred square

Ten lots of ten make one **hundred**.

100 **pence**

1	2	3	4	5	6	7	8	9	10
11	12	13	14	15	16	17	18	19	20
21	22	23	24	25	26	27	28	29	30
31	32	33	34	35	36	37	38	39	40
41	42	43	44	45	46	47	48	49	50
51	52	53	54	55	56	57	58	59	60
61	62	63	64	65	66	67	68	69	70
71	72	73	74	75	76	77	78	79	80
81	82	83	84	85	86	87	88	89	90
91	92	93	94	95	96	97	98	99	100

One **hundred square**.

kilogram

A **kilogram** is a **measure** of **weight**.

kg is short for kilogram.
A kilogram is 1000 **grams**.

length

The **length** of a line or object is the distance from one end to the other.

6cm

The length an event can also be measured.

1 hour

lunchtime starts

lunchtime ends

less, least

Less or **least** is the smaller or smallest **number** or amount.

4 is less than 7. The spoon **weighs** less than the bowl.

John has saved less than Sarah.
Syeda has saved less than John.
Syeda has saved the least.

light, lighter, lightest

Light means having little **weight**.

A feather is light.

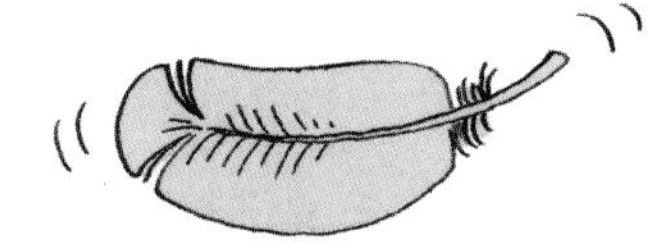

The cat is **lighter** than the dog.
The rabbit is lighter than the cat.
The rabbit is the **lightest**.

line

A **line** is drawn from one point to another.
It has length but no width. It can be **straight** or **curved**.

litre

You use **litres** to **measure** amounts of liquids.
A litre is a measure of **capacity**.

l is short for litre.
A litre is 1000 **millilitres**.

long, longer, longest

See also: metre

Long, longer, longest describe **length**.

12 centimetres

The pink toothbrush is 12 **centimetres long**.
The pink toothbrush is **longer** than the blue toothbrush.
The yellow toothbrush is the **longest**.

measure, measuring scale

You **measure** things to find out their size.
Length, weight, capacity and time are different kinds of measure.

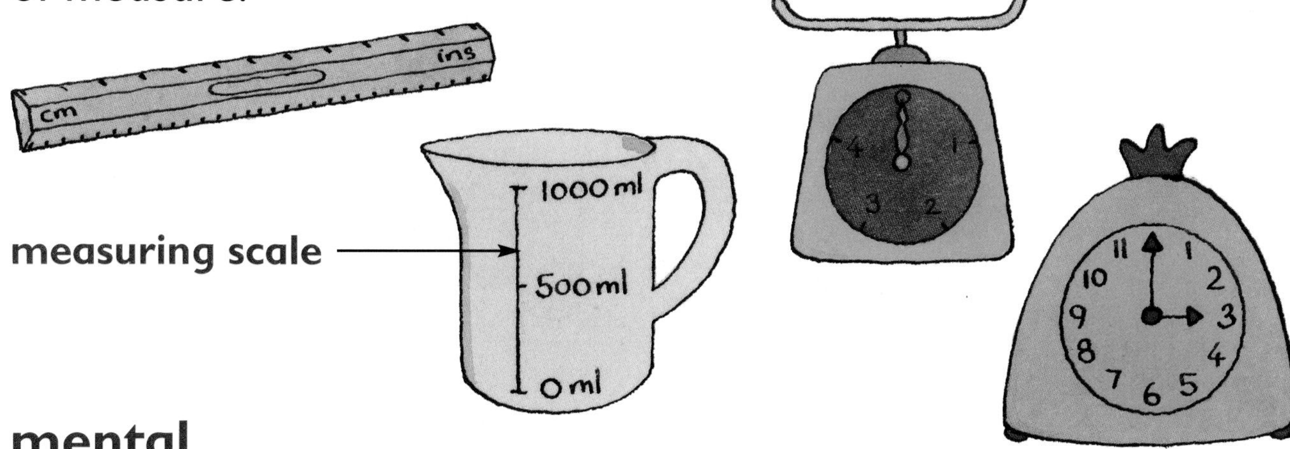

mental

Mental means 'in your head'.
You do mental **calculations** in your head.

metre, metre stick

A **metre** is a **measure** of **length**.
A metre is 100 **centimetres**.

m is short for metre.

Metre sticks help you measure how **long** things are.
The giraffe is 5 metres **tall.**

0 10 20 30 40 50 60 70 80 90 100

1m = 100 cm

a
b
c
d
e
f
g
h
i
j
k
l
m
n
o
p
q
r
s
t
u
v
w
x
y
z

midday

Midday is 12 o'clock in the daytime.
It is the end of the morning, and the start of the afternoon.

midnight

Midnight is 12 o'clock at night.
It is the end of one **day,**
and the start of the next.

millilitre

You use **millilitres** to **measure** amounts of liquids.
A millilitre is a measure of **capacity**.

ml is short for millilitre.
1000 millilitres is a **litre**.

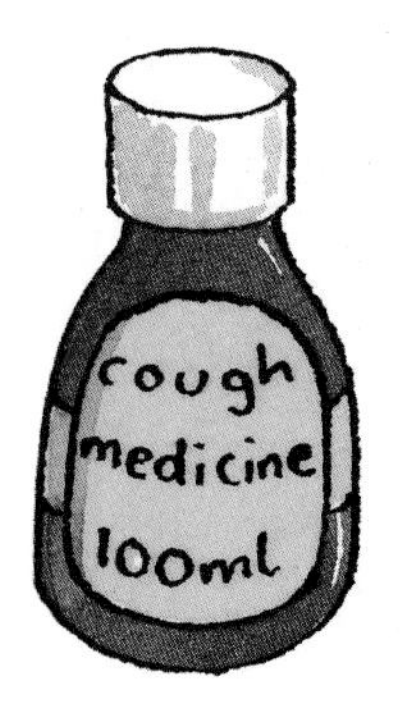

5 ml

minus

– This is a **minus** sign.
It means **'subtract'** or 'take away'.

Six minus four **equals** two.

minute

A **minute** is a short **measure** of time.
A minute is 60 **seconds**.
There are 60 minutes in an **hour**.

month

There are 12 **months** in a **year**.
There are 28, 29, 30 or 31 **days** in a month.

a b c d e f g h i j k l m n o p q r s t u v w x y z

more, most

More or **most** is the greater or greatest **number** or amount.

5 is more than 3.

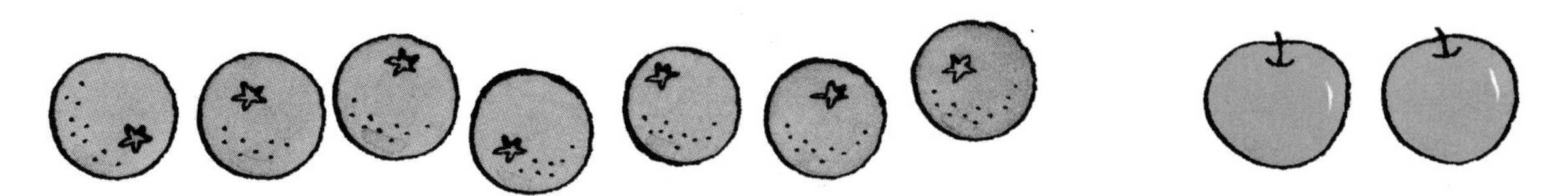

There are more oranges than apples.

Kim has most tomatoes.
Ravi has most eggs.
John has most chips.

multiple

When you **multiply** two numbers together,
the answer is a **multiple**.

1	x	2	=	2
2	x	2	=	4
3	x	2	=	6
4	x	2	=	8
5	x	2	=	10
6	x	2	=	12
7	x	2	=	14
8	x	2	=	16
9	x	2	=	18
10	x	2	=	20

The multiples of 2.

1	x	5	=	5
2	x	5	=	10
3	x	5	=	15
4	x	5	=	20
5	x	5	=	25
6	x	5	=	30
7	x	5	=	35
8	x	5	=	40
9	x	5	=	45
10	x	5	=	50

The multiples of 5.

multiply, multiplied by, multiplication

See also: operation

You **multiply** when you find how many things there are in a number of same-size groups.

X This is a **multiplication** sign.
It means 'times', 'lots of' or '**multiplied by**'.

Three lots of two.
Three times two.
Three twos.

3 x 2

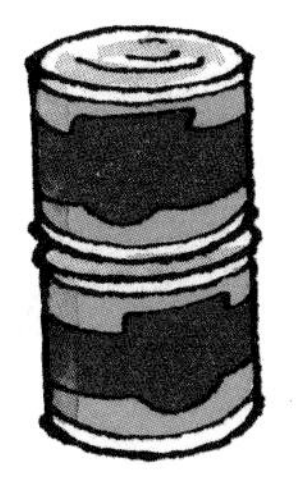
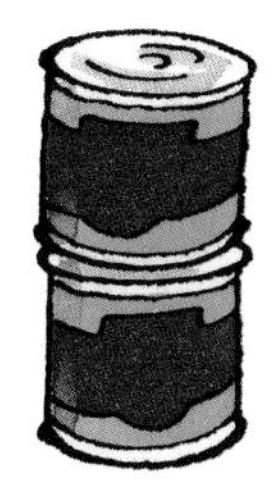
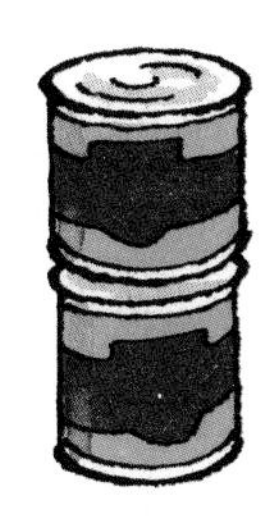

Five lots of three.
Five times three.
Five threes.

5 x 3

Multiplication is the opposite of **division**.

nought

Nought means nothing or **zero**.
It is written as a **0**

number, numeral

Numbers are used for counting.
They tell you how many there are of something.
Numbers can be written as **numerals**.

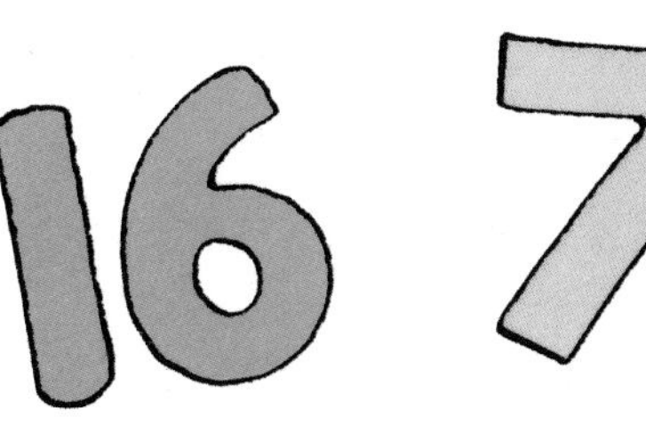

a b c d e f g h i j k l m n o p q r s t u v w x y z

number line

A **number line** shows the correct order of a group of **numbers**.

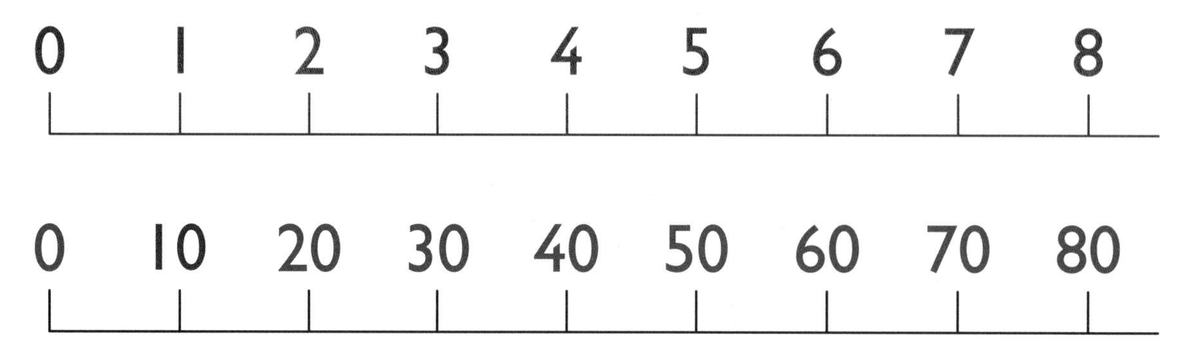

octagon

An **octagon** has 8 **straight sides** and 8 **corners**.

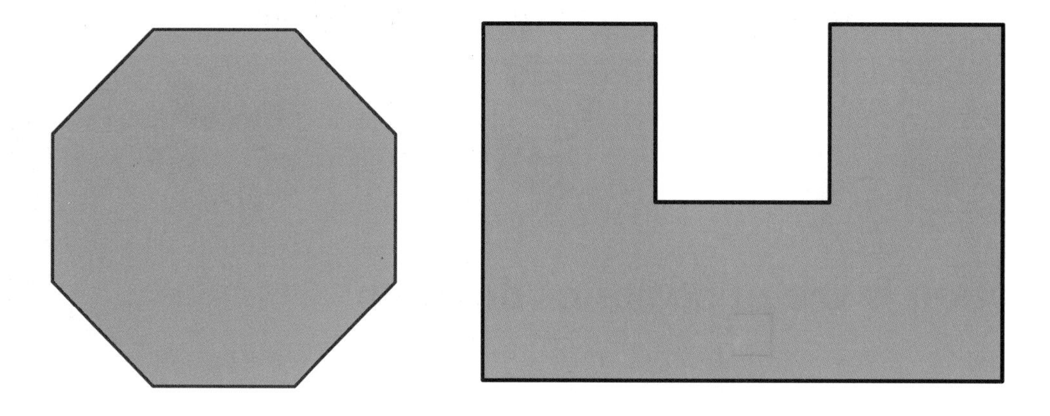

odd number

An **odd number** cannot be **divided** exactly by two.

1, 3, 5, 7, 9, 11, 13, . . . are odd numbers.

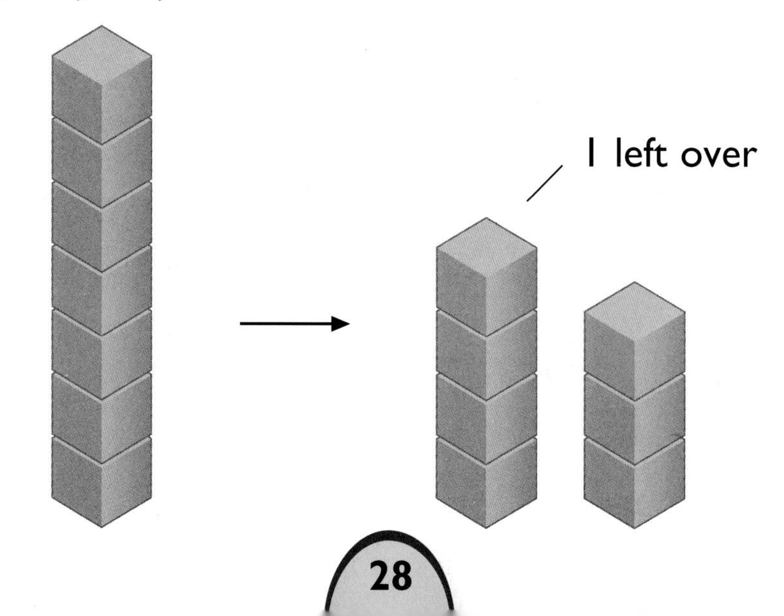

operation, operation sign

Add, subtract, multiply and **divide** are all **operations**.

These are **operation signs**.

pair

A **pair** is a set of two things that go together.

pattern

A **pattern** is an arrangement of **numbers** or shapes.
Patterns often repeat themselves.

Finding a pattern in a **sequence** of numbers or shapes helps you to work out what comes next or what is missing.

1 4 ... 10 13 16

The pattern is '**add** 3 each time'. 7 is missing.

penny, pence

A **penny** is a small amount of money.
Pennies are often called **pence**.

1p is short for one penny or one pence.
There are 100 pennies in a **pound**.

1p coins

pentagon

A **pentagon** has 5 **straight sides** and 5 **corners**.

pictogram

A **pictogram** shows information using pictures or symbols. Each picture or symbol stands for an amount. This is shown in a key.

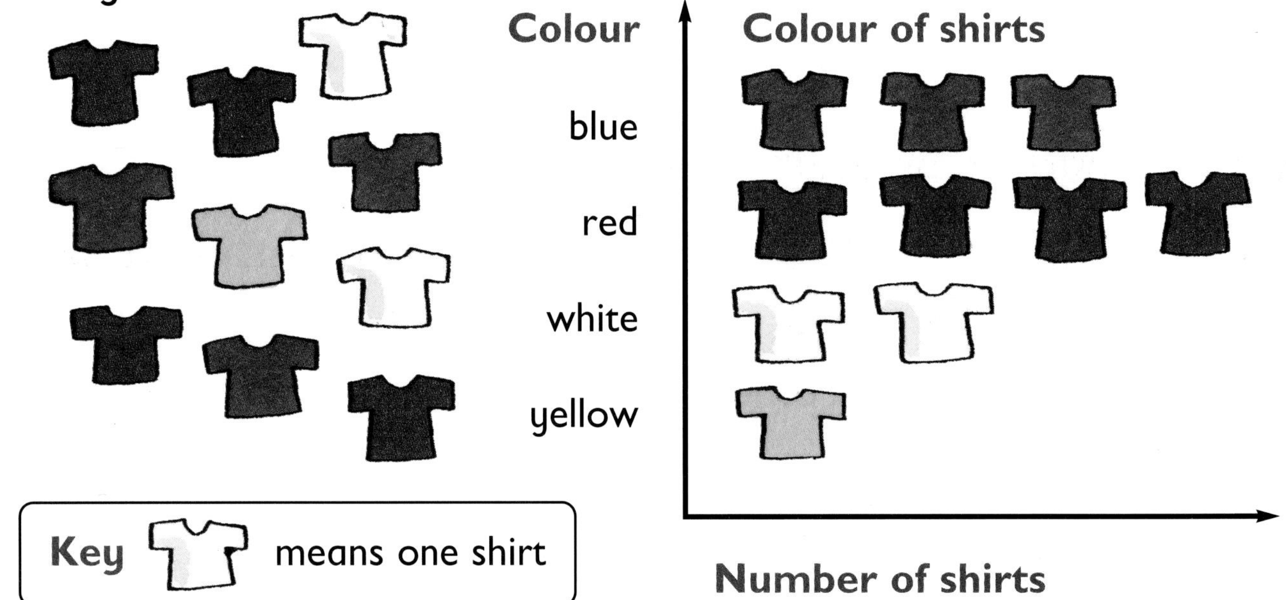

place value

The **place value** of a **digit** is how much it is worth.

In the number **361**

the digit 3 means 3 hundreds

the digit 6 means 6 tens

the digit 1 means 1 unit.

H	T	U
3	6	1

plus

+ This is a **plus** sign.
It means '**add**'.

Two plus five **equals** seven.

Six plus four equals ten.

point

A **point** marks a place or position.

This arrow shows the point where 9 would be.

0 number line 10

pound

A **pound** is an amount of money.
One pound is 100 **pennies** or **pence**.

£6 is short for six pounds.

£1 coins

price

The **price** of an object is how much money it costs.

pyramid

A **pyramid** is a **solid** shape. The bottom of a pyramid can be any shape with **straight sides**. The other **faces** are **triangles** and meet at a **point**.

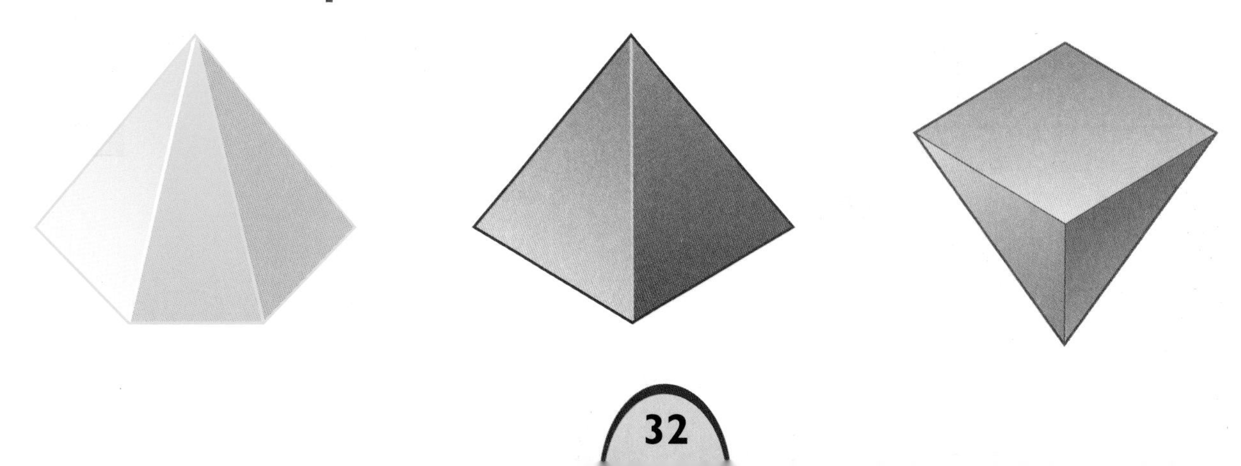

quarter

See also: quarter past, quarter to, quarter turn

A **quarter** is a **fraction**. There are four quarters in a whole.

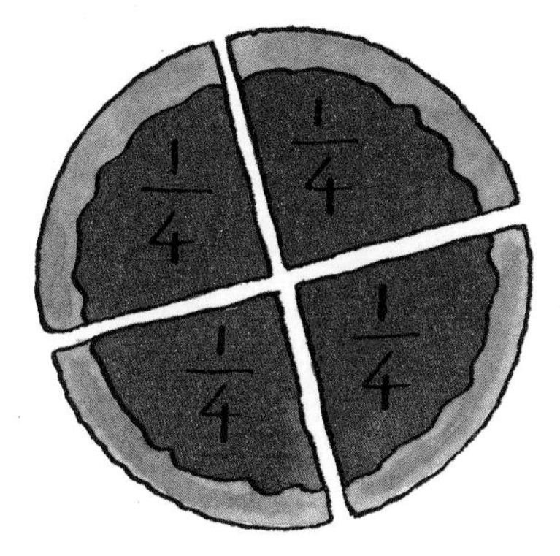

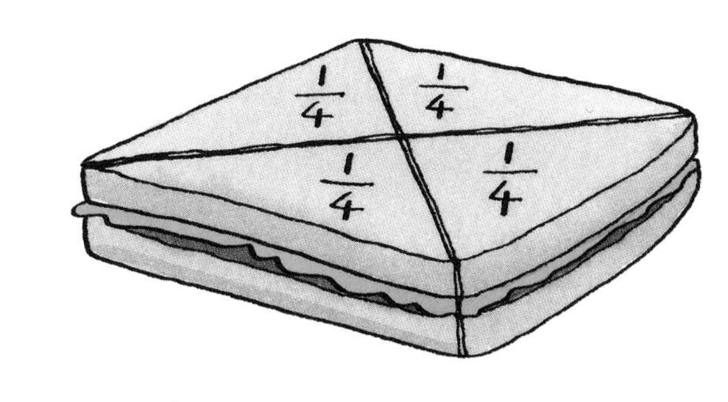

If you **divide** something into four equal parts, each part is a quarter.

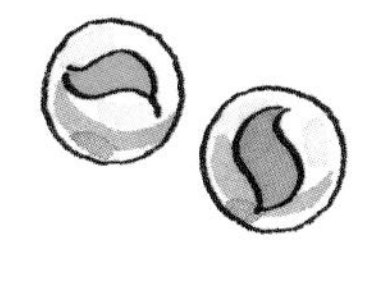
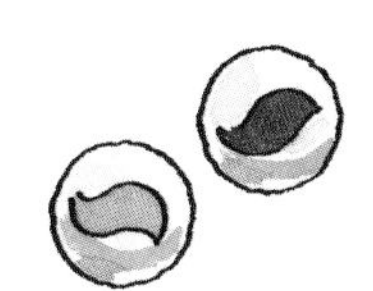
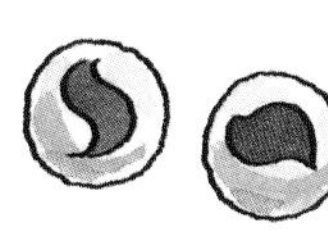

A quarter of 8 is 2.

quarter past

A **quarter** of the **hour** has past.
It is 15 **minutes** past the hour.

quarter past one

quarter to

There is a **quarter** of an **hour** until the next 'o'clock'.
It is 45 **minutes** past the hour.

quarter to five

quarter turn

A **quarter turn** is a **quarter** of a **whole turn**.
One quarter turn is a **right angle**.
Four quarter turns make one whole turn.

rectangle, rectangular

A **rectangle** has 4 straight **sides** and 4 **corners.**
It has a **right angle** at each corner.

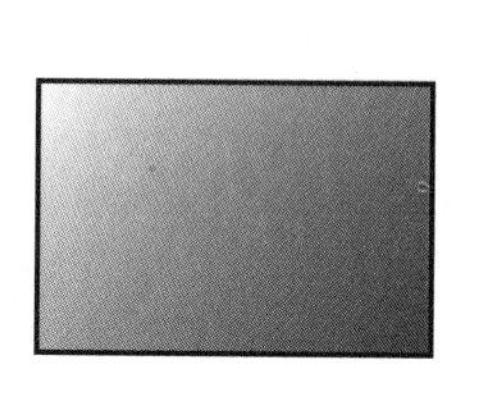

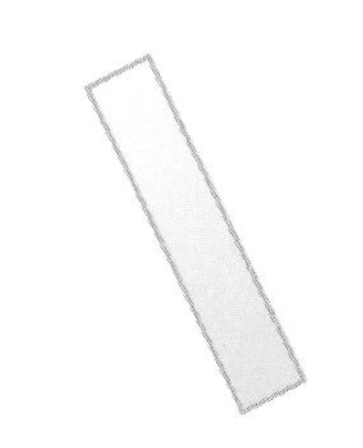

These paintings are **rectangular**.
They are rectangle shaped.

reflection

A **reflection** is what you see in a mirror.
One side of a **symmetrical** shape is a reflection of the other.

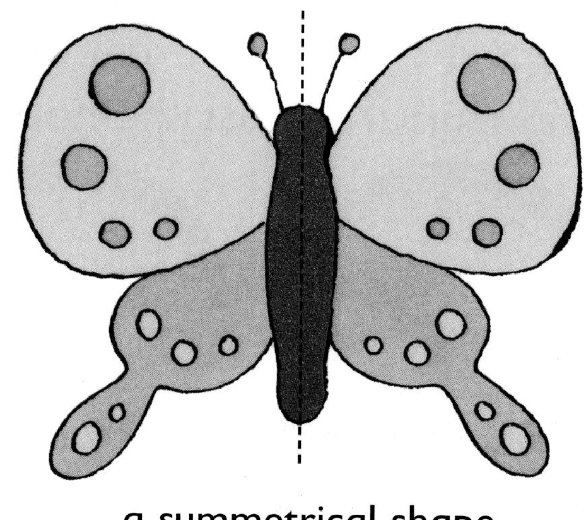

a symmetrical shape

right angle

A **right angle** is one **quarter turn**.
Each **corner** of a **rectangle** is a right angle.

round

See also: estimate

You can **round** a **number** to its nearest **multiple** of 10, or 100.

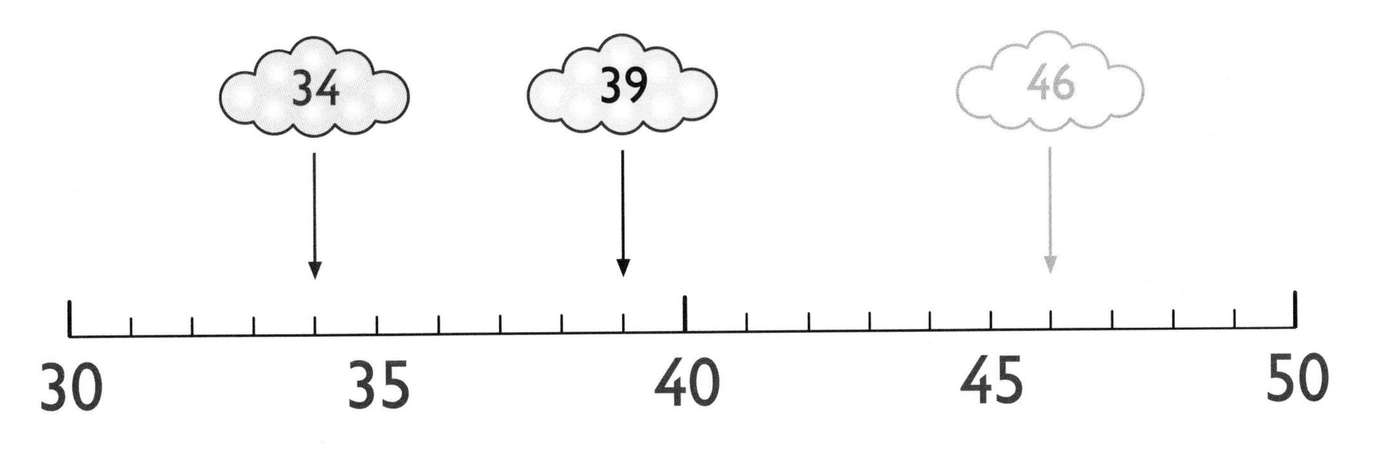

34 rounds down to 30. 39 rounds up to 40. 46 rounds up to 50.

a b c d e f g h i j k l m n o p q r s t u v w x y z

row See also: array

A **row** is a line of objects or **numbers**, side by side.

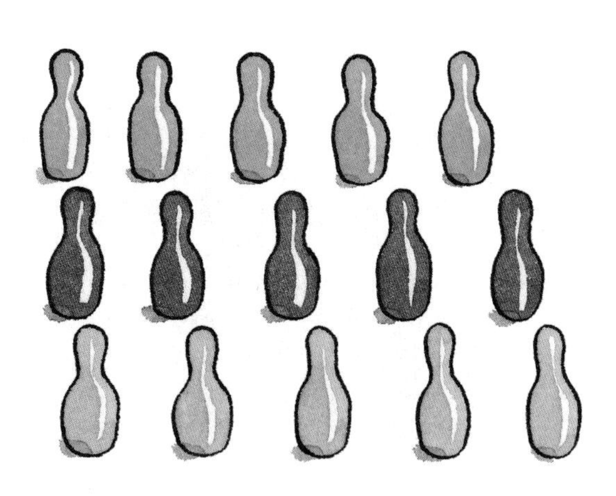

3 rows of skittles.

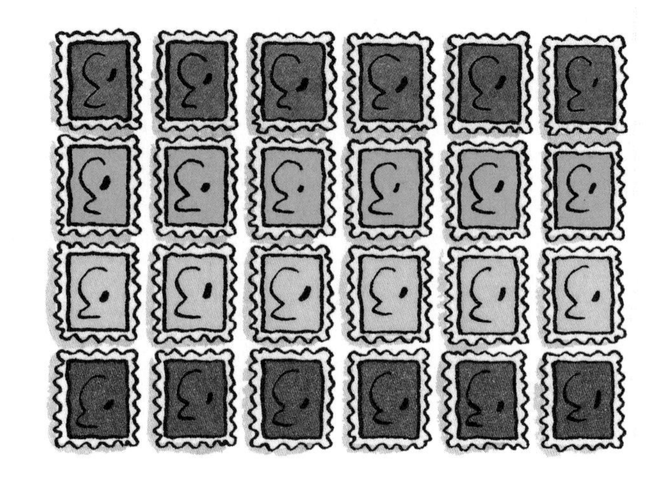

4 rows of stamps.

ruler

A **ruler** is a **straight edge** with a **measuring scale** marked on it.
You can use a ruler to draw a straight **line**.

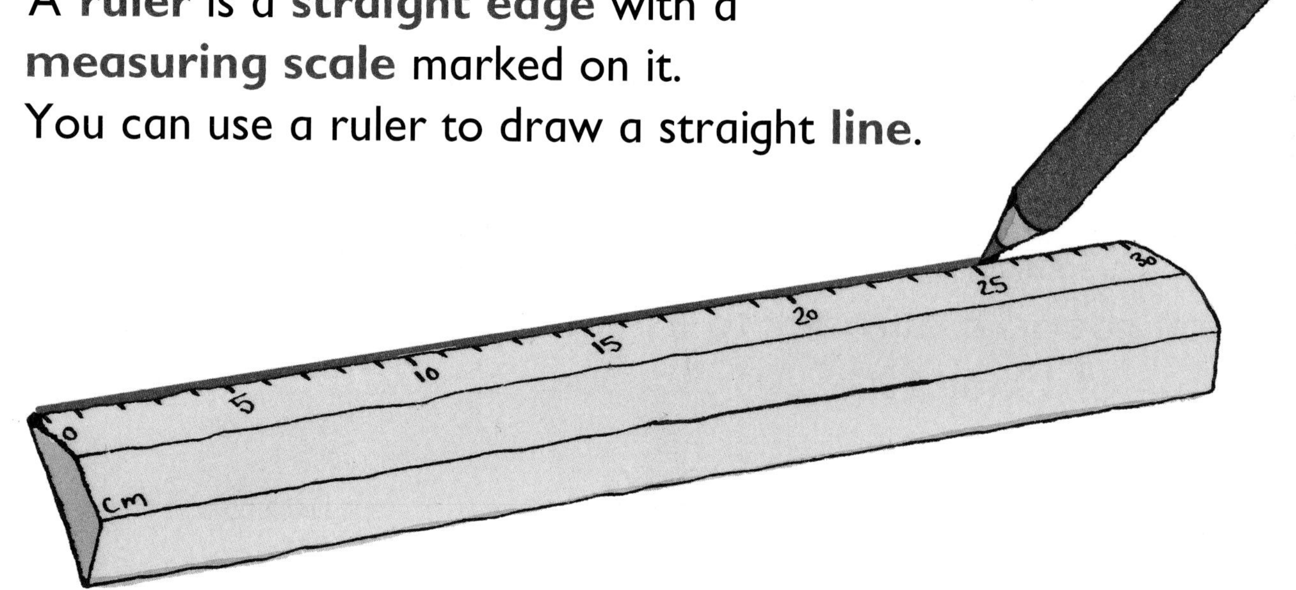

You can use a ruler to **measure length**.

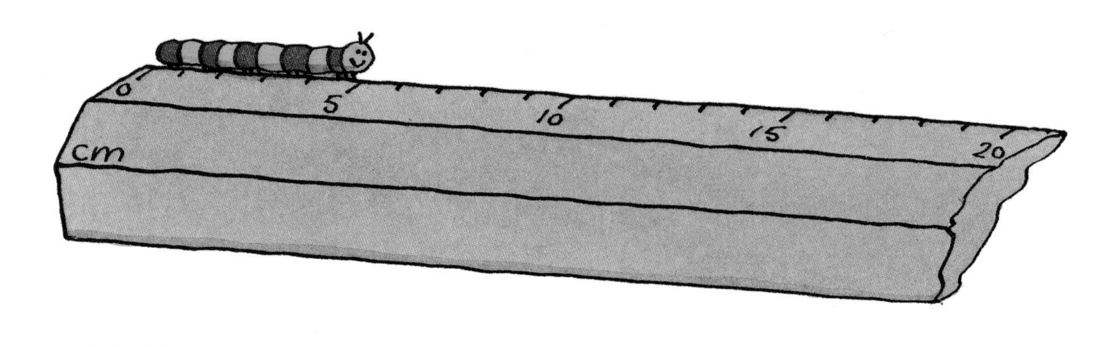

season

Seasons name the time of the **year**.
There are 4 seasons.

second

A **second** is a very short **measure** of time.
There are 60 seconds in a **minute**.

Some watches have a hand that counts the seconds.

sequence

A **sequence** is a **set** of **numbers** or shapes with a **pattern**.

1 3 5 7 9 ...

2 4 6 8 10 ...

5 10 15 20 25 ...

...

set

A **set** is a group of **numbers**, shapes or objects that are alike in some way.

short, shorter, shortest

Short, shorter, shortest describe **length**.

The white straw and the green straw are short.
The pink straw is shorter than the blue straw.
The green straw is the shortest.

side **See also: corner**

Flat shapes have **sides**.
Sides can be **straight** or **curved**.

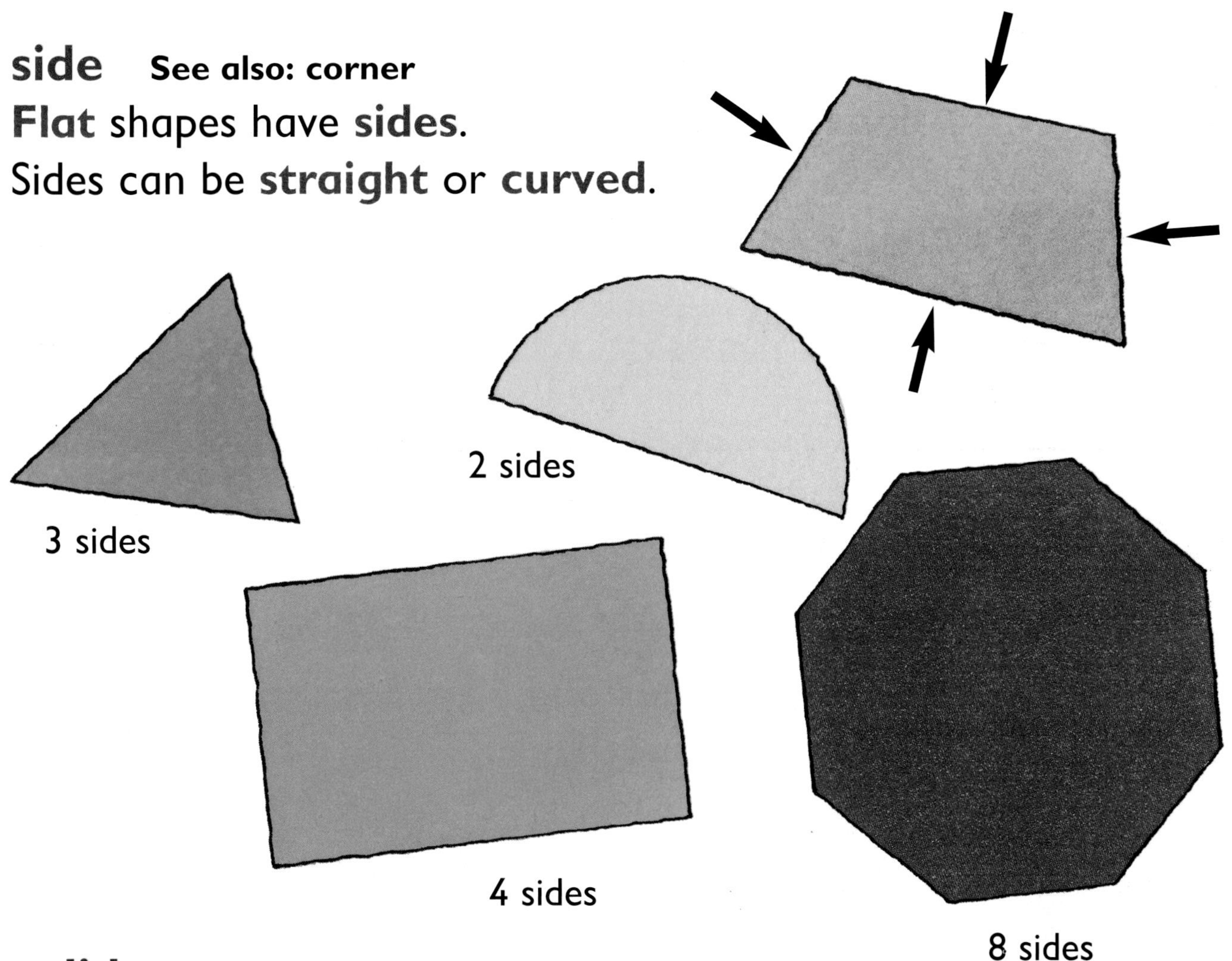

solid **See also: edge, face, corner**

These are **solid** shapes.
There is no space inside.

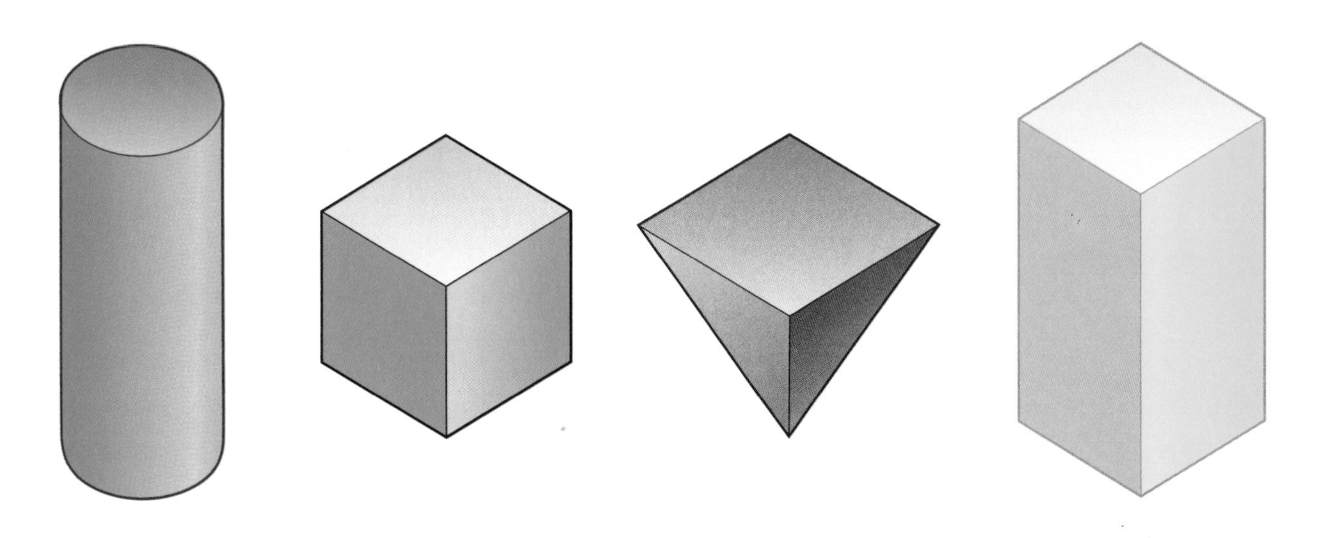

sphere

A **sphere** is perfectly round, like a ball.

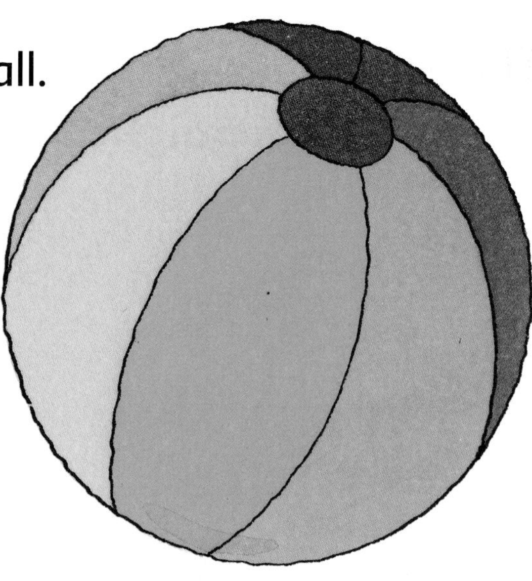

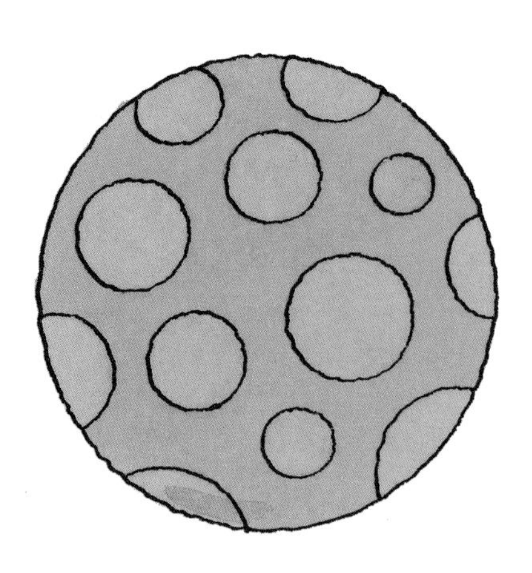

square

See also: rectangle

A **square** has 4 **straight sides** and 4 **corners**.
All the sides are the same **length**.
All the corners are **right angles**.

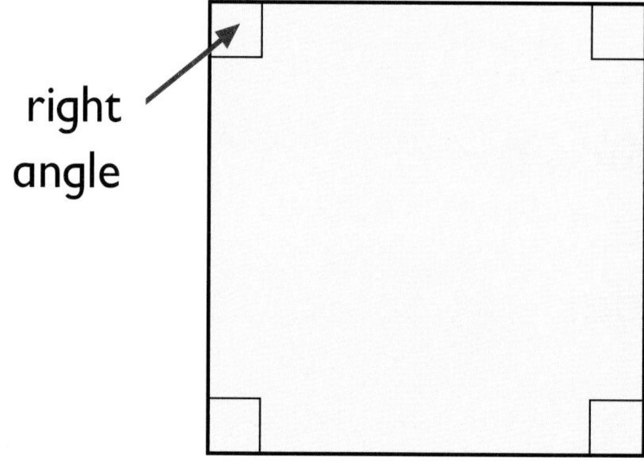

star

A star is a **flat** shape with several points.

A five-pointed star.

A six-pointed star.

straight

These **lines** are all **straight**.

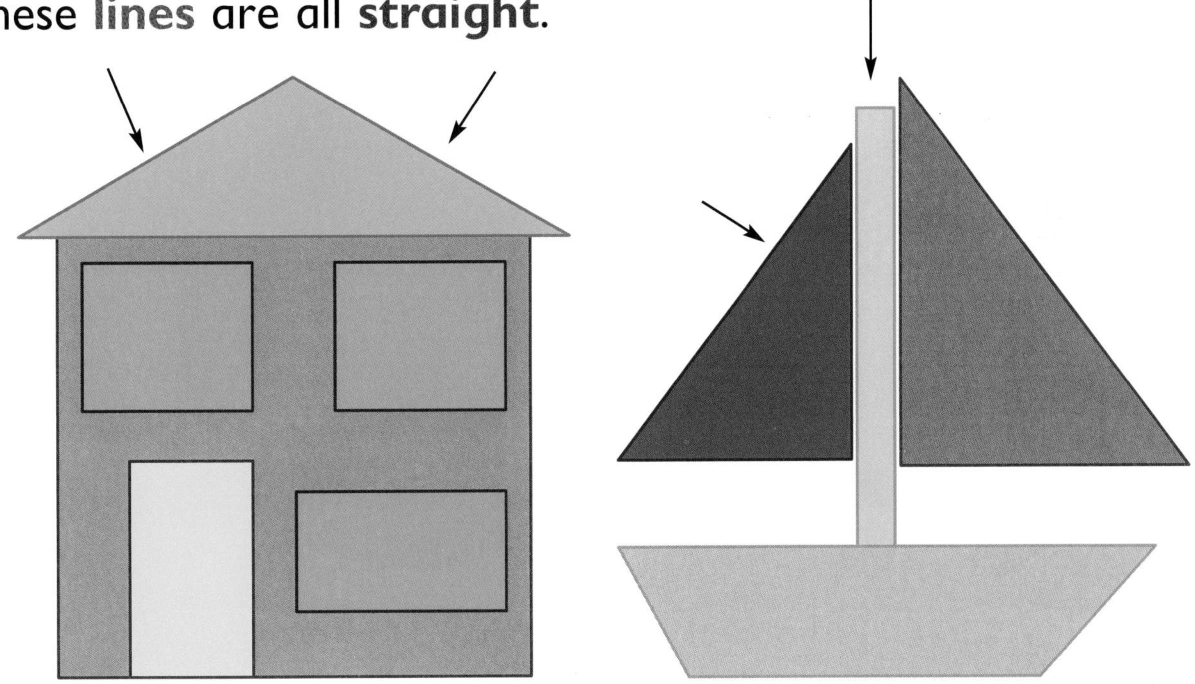

subtract, subtraction

See also: operation

We **subtract** when we take away and see how many are left.
Subtract means 'take away' or '**minus**'.

Five take away
two leaves three.

5 – 2 = 3

Six **minus** one leaves five.

6 – 1 = 5

These are **subtractions**.
Subtraction is the opposite of **addition**.

a
b
c
d
e
f
g
h
i
j
k
l
m
n
o
p
q
r
s
t
u
v
w
x
y
z

surface

The **surface** is the outside part of a shape.

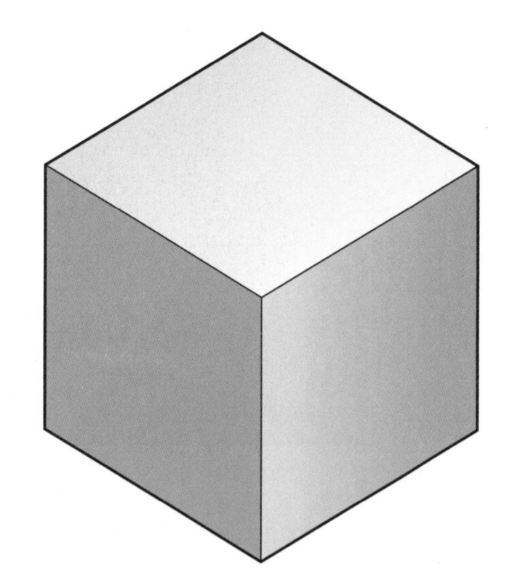

The **cube** has a **flat** surface.

The **sphere** has a **curved** surface.

symmetry, symmetrical

See also: reflection

Symmetrical shapes can be folded so that one side fits exactly on top of the other.
The fold **line** is the line of **symmetry**.

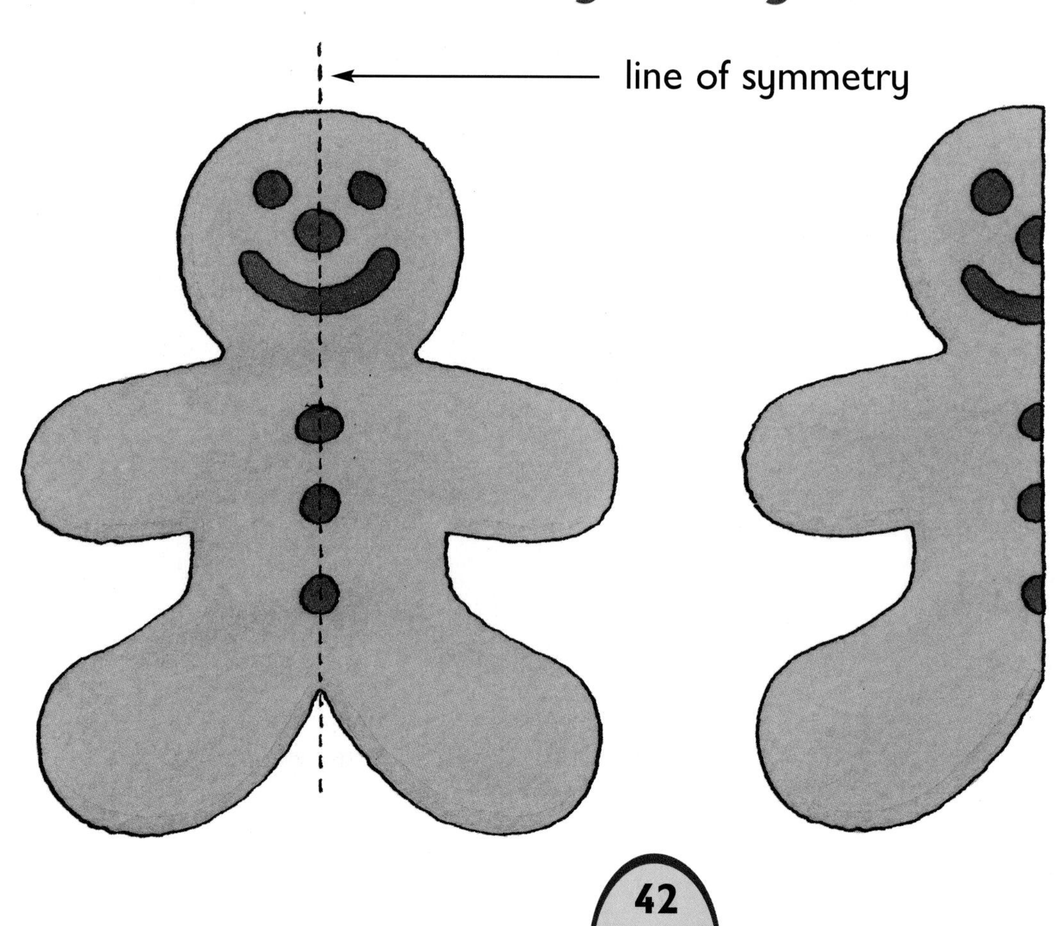

tall, taller, tallest

Tall is used to describe height.

The monsters are tall.

The blue monster is 3 **metres** tall.
The red monster is **taller** than the blue monster.
The yellow monster is the **tallest**.

tape measure

A **tape measure** helps you find out the **length** of objects.
It is marked with **centimetres** and **metres**.

thousand

One **thousand** is the name for ten **hundreds**.

… 991 992 993 994 995 996 997 998 999 **1000**

three-digit number

These are **three-digit numbers**.

They each have three **digits**: a **hundreds** digit, a tens digit and a **units** digit.

153 ⟶ 1 hundred, 5 tens and 3 units

times table

These are **times tables**. The answers are **multiples**.

Times two table x 2 table	Times five table x 5 table	Times ten table x 10 table
1 x 2 = 2	1 x 5 = 5	1 x 10 = 10
2 x 2 = 4	2 x 5 = 10	2 x 10 = 20
3 x 2 = 6	3 x 5 = 15	3 x 10 = 30
4 x 2 = 8	4 x 5 = 20	4 x 10 = 40
5 x 2 = 10	5 x 5 = 25	5 x 10 = 50
6 x 2 = 12	6 x 5 = 30	6 x 10 = 60
7 x 2 = 14	7 x 5 = 35	7 x 10 = 70
8 x 2 = 16	8 x 5 = 40	8 x 10 = 80
9 x 2 = 18	9 x 5 = 45	9 x 10 = 90
10 x 2 = 20	10 x 5 = 50	10 x 10 = 100

tomorrow

Tomorrow is the day after today.
If today is Monday, tomorrow is Tuesday.

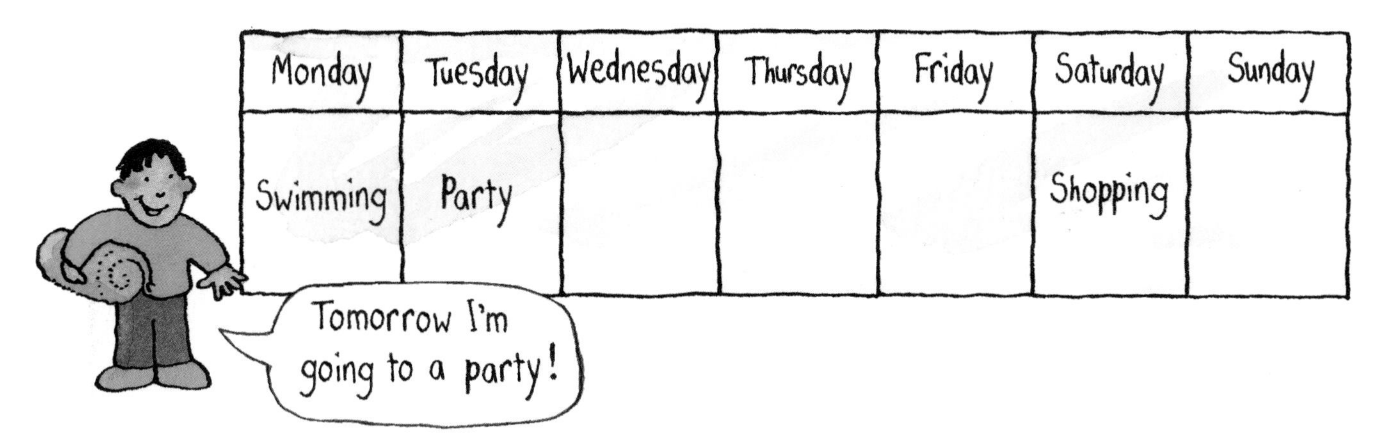

Monday	Tuesday	Wednesday	Thursday	Friday	Saturday	Sunday
Swimming	Party				Shopping	

total

The **total** is the answer to an **addition**.

20p + 10p + 5p = 35p

Total: 35p

Total: 7

triangle, triangular

A **triangle** has 3 **straight sides** and 3 **corners**.

These signs are **triangular**.
They are triangle shaped.

a
b
c
d
e
f
g
h
i
j
k
l
m
n
o
p
q
r
s
t
u
v
w
x
y
z

twice **See also: double**

Twice means two times.

The dog barks twice.

A six is thrown twice.

two-digit number

These are **two-digit numbers**.
They each have two **digits**:
a tens digit and a **units** digit.

35 ⟶ 3 tens and 5 units

unit

A **unit** is one thing or object.
In a **number** the units **digit** tells how many ones or units there are.

48 ⟶ 4 tens and 8 units

week **See also: fortnight, weekend, year**

A **week** is 7 **days**.

weekend

The **weekend** is Saturday and Sunday.
You do not go to school on these **days**.

Monday	Tuesday	Wednesday	Thursday	Friday	Saturday	Sunday

weigh, weight

You **weigh** something to find out how **heavy** it is.
You are finding its **weight**.
A force called gravity gives you weight.

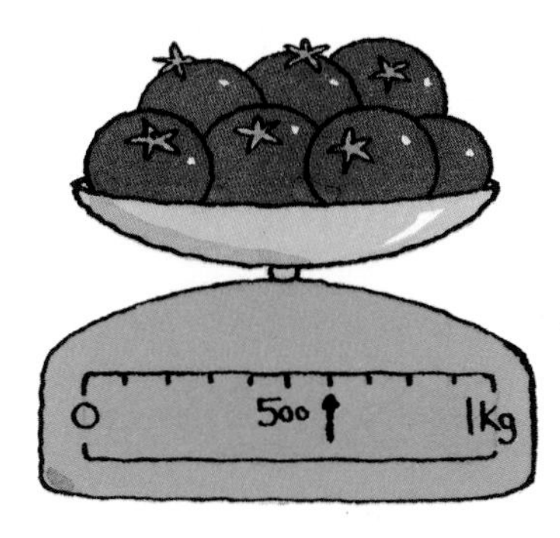

The tomatoes weigh 600 **grams**.

The cat weighs 4 **kilograms**.

whole turn **See also: half turn, quarter turn**

A **whole turn** goes all the way round,
and comes back to where it started.

The rides make lots
of whole turns.

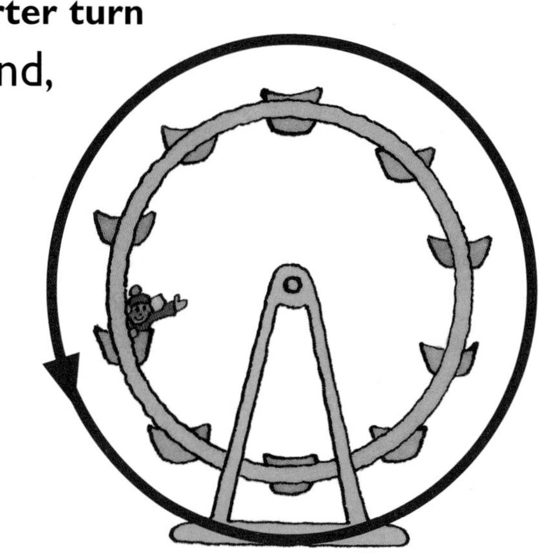

year

A **year** is 12 **months.**
A year is 52 **weeks.**
A year is 365 **days.**
There are 4 **seasons** in a year.

Simon is 6 years old.

BIRTHDAYS

January	February	March
Chloe, Simon, Lucy	Saif, Emily	Paul, Josh, Holly
April	**May**	**June**
Mia, Jack	Zoe, Ravi, Ellie	Sam, Megan
July	**August**	**September**
Liam, Amy	Alex, Sarah	Sophie, Mark, Lena
October	**November**	**December**
Laura, Tim	Luke, Zoe	Jade, Tom

yesterday

Yesterday was the **day** before today.
If today is Friday, yesterday was Thursday.

zero

Zero means **nought** or nothing.

It is written as **0**.